I'm just Ryan

First published in 2024 by OH
An Imprint of HEADLINE PUBLISHING GROUP

1

Disclaimer:

Cataloguing in Publication Data is available from the British Library

ISBN 978-1-03542-233-3

Compiled and written by: Malcolm Croft
Editorial: Matt Tomlinson
Designed by: Stephen Cary
Project manager: Russell Porter
Illustration by: Ryan Adley
Production: Arlene Lestrade
Printed and bound in Dubai

MIX
Paper | Supporting responsible forestry
FSC® C104740
www.fsc.org

Headline's policy is to use papers that are natural, renewable and recyclable products and made from wood grown in well-managed forests and other controlled sources. The logging and manufacturing processes are expected to conform to the environmental regulations of the country of origin.

HEADLINE PUBLISHING GROUP
An Hachette UK Company
Carmelite House, 50 Victoria Embankment, London EC4Y 0DZ

www.headline.co.uk   www.hachette.co.uk

I'm just Ryan

THE LITTLE GUIDE TO
RYAN GOSLING
UNOFFICIAL AND UNAUTHORIZED

CONTENTS

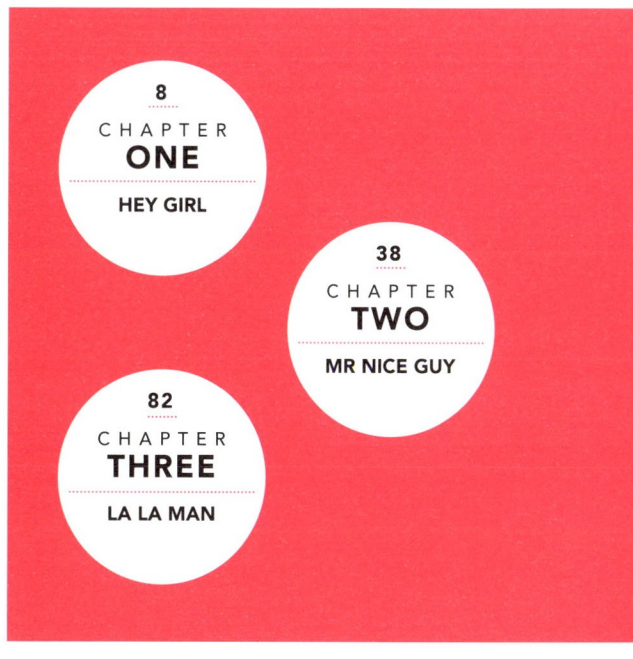

INTRODUCTION

Twenty-odd years ago, former Disney Mousketeer turned offbeat indie outsider Ryan Gosling glowed up from an ugly young goose – a gosling! – to a super-sexy swan when he headlined his first proper Hollywood flick, *The Notebook*, in 2004. (OK, Ryan has never, ever, ever been ugly, but you get the picture.)

Ever since, Ryan has taken his rocketing career on a long and winding drive filled with sweeping twists and turns, with each new film often as surprising, and shocking, as the last. From his penetrating, brooding brutality in the thriller *Drive*, to his heart-throbbing hunk in the romantic comedy *Crazy, Stupid, Love*, to his magical, melodic fingering on the piano in the musical *La La Land,* to breathing life – and Kenergy – into a patriarchy-plagued plastic doll in the fantasy dramedy *Barbie*, no other actor in recent times can boast a resumé as remarkable and ridiculous as Ryan's. It's little wonder that he is now Hollywood's most in-demand star player, a man twice as talented as he is handsome.

(Which doesn't seem fair, really, when you think about it.) Put simply: there is no one quite like Ryan Gosling.

This little guide revels in all things Ryan-related. It's a gentle reminder of his 20-year anniversary since his first rise to superstardom, and a tiny celebratory tome filled with all of his greatest oddball wit, wisdom and bon mots, which, if you've ever seen him crack wise or tell a joke, you'll know is a lot. This little handheld slice of Ryan Gosling is the perfect bedtime snuggle companion, a compact compendium that provides the perfect daily dose of *Goslingology*, as we've coined it, a quick pick-me-up guide to how to be more like Ryan that you won't ever want to put down.

So, what are we waiting for? Let's go get our Gosling on…

Word of warning: this book contains more than a few swoon-worthy quotes and quips, so make sure you're sitting down before you tuck in.

CHAPTER
ONE

Hey Girl

Way, way back at the start of the 1990s, "Canada's first ever Disney Mouseketeer" Ryan Gosling was "dryhumping" (his words, not ours) his way to day time TV fame when he was just 12 years old.

However, all was not easy for this overly confident but awkward entertainer. He battled monsters and demons at school and at home long before he did as the titular *Young Hercules*.

Let's flashback to where all good origin stories start – with a troubled young hero looking for an adventure…

> **"**
> I didn't have an arthouse cinema
> in my town, so films did not
> mirror life. Instead, they were
> a portal to another world.
> **"**

Ryan, on blockbuster movies and his local multiplex
cinema, interview with Jonathan Dean, *The Sunday
Times*, April 28, 2024.

66

When I was a kid it was a big deal to go to the movies. And when the movie was no good I was really disappointed for the whole week. So I wanna give people their money's worth, and with *Lars and the Real Girl* we've done that. You've never seen anything like this.

99

Ryan Gosling, on *Lars and the Real Girl* and the importance of making a good movie, interview with Jack Foley, London.net, March 14, 2008.

My biggest influence was my uncle. He moved in with us when I was a kid and became an Elvis impersonator. Watching him become that character, watching him become someone else, watching the way it brought the best out of everybody. I wanted to find some way to be around that energy. So I joined a dance company for a while. And then films began having an impact on me.

Ryan, on his uncle's Elvis impersonation act as his biggest creative inspiration, interview with Jessica Hundley, *Time Out*, May 2, 2016.

My sister [Mandi] and I used to sing at weddings. We would sing 'When a Man Loves a Woman' to the bride. While the bride was sitting on the chair, I would get down on my knees and sing. My work as a wedding singer landed me a spot in my uncle's Elvis impersonator act – his name was Perry, and he went by 'Elvis Perry'.

Ryan, on his earliest performances and the origins of his desire to entertain, interview with Steve Carrell, *Interview*, October 7, 2010.

66

I was a schmuck. I didn't feel very smart. They kept passing me in school even though I didn't know how to do things I should have known how to do. I couldn't read. When you're in class and you can't read and everyone else can, it's pretty frustrating. I couldn't absorb any of the information, so I caused trouble.

99

Ryan, on struggling to stay focused at school and causing trouble with teachers and classmates, interview with Dave Karger, *Entertainment Weekly*, April 20, 2007.

I related to Lars more than any other character I have ever played. I had a terrible time at school too. I think that hopefully everyone can relate to him. We all share those qualities, although his are amplified and it manifests itself in a more creative way. But I think that we all feel isolated, that we all have trouble communicating who we are to people. We all get social anxieties.

Ryan, on his bond with his character Lars, from *Lars and the Real Girl*, interview with movies.ie, March 2007.

As a kid, when I was walking to school I saw this guy on a motorcycle get hit by a car. And this motorcycle guy was there just lying in the middle of the street. I went up to him and he had blood coming from behind his head. My first thought was: I've got to get a motorcycle.

Ryan, on his love of anything with wheels, interview with Will Lawrence, *The Telegraph*, April 4, 2013.

I started ninety-five percent
of the fights, and I just
happened to lose them all.
My mother took me out
of school because I wasn't
doing well. She quit her job,
and taught me at home.

Ryan, on how he got his nickname "Trouble" at school,
interview with Michael Martin, *VMAN*, September 2005.

I saw Raquel Welch on *The Muppet Show* when I was young. She was dressed like a cavewoman. She was dancing with a big puppet spider, and I liked it. I liked it more than anything I'd ever liked before.

Ryan, on his first ever celebrity cinematic crush, interview with Lynn Hirschberg, *W Magazine*, January 3, 2024.

66

It was kind of obvious early on that Mormonism wasn't going to suit the life that I wanted. My mother [Donna] is somebody who really appreciates the individual, and she really supported me. My mother and sister [Mandi] are still very religious, and it really works for them.

99

Ryan, on rejecting his parents' religion, interview with Michael Martin, *VMAN*, September 2005.

17,000

The number of fellow young actors and dancers auditioning alongside Ryan for a spot on Disney's *All-New Mickey Mouse Club* TV show in 1993.

He won the sacred spot after wowing Disney with his rather erotic dance routine he called "The Move".

I hated being a kid. A lot of kids feel like they got forced into being a child actor, but I wanted it, because I wanted to be an adult.

Ryan, on his disdain for having to be a kid, interview with Alex Pappademas, *GQ*, October 9, 2007.

I didn't play sports at school, so my parents got in touch with this woman who had a dance company. I worked with the company for two years. I thought, 'I'll do this, it's great, there are girls everywhere.' Then there was this thing in the paper calling for young people who could dance. I went and ended up getting the job. It was for the *Mickey Mouse Club*.

Ryan, on how his love of dancing (and girls) got him his first audition at age 12 for the *Mickey Mouse Club* TV show, interview with Michael Martin, *VMAN*, September 2005.

Up onstage I start dry-humping. I'm grabbing my stuff, I'm licking my fingers, I'm going up to grown women and trying to grind their faces. I'm seven years old. And I won! And I got on the front page of the newspaper. I got kinda famous for it. I got beat up a lot for it, too. But it was worth it because I knew it was my ticket outta there. I thought, 'If I could show this move to America I could build an empire'. So I go to the *Mickey Mouse Club* audition, and I do 'The Move' – and I get on the show.

Ryan, on his first taste of fame at a local talent show in the 1990s from doing his "inherently filthy" dance routine called "The Move", interview with Alex Pappademas, *GQ*, 2007.

I would do these super-sexual moves. Disney confused my inappropriateness for talent, and once they realized there was no more I could do, it was too late.

Ryan, on winning his spot on Disney's *All-New Mickey Mouse Club* with his erotic dance routine, interview with Rebecca Winters Keegan, *Time*, October 4, 2007.

I certainly wasn't a child prodigy.
Everyone else was. I didn't know why
I was there. And it's why I didn't
work. They dressed me up as a
hamster or put me in the background
of someone's song. It was all a great
experience in a way because it helped
me figure out what I wasn't going
to be good at.

Ryan, on his two-year tenure on Disney's *The All-New Mickey Mouse Club*, interview with Zach Baron, *GQ*, May 31, 2023.

The Mickey Mouse Club was kind of depressing when I got there because they realized that I wasn't really up to snuff in comparison with what some of the other kids were able to do… I would just come in at the beginning of the show and then come back at the end, and occasionally I'd have a sketch here or there, but I didn't end up working that much, which was disheartening.

Ryan, on his time at *The All-New Mickey Mouse Club*, interview with Steve Carrell, *Interview*, October 7, 2010.

I had my hustle. It was whatever I could do to not end up working in a factory. If I had to shake it like a showgirl, I was going to do it.

Ryan, on doing whatever it took to get on TV in his *Mickey Mouse Club* days, interview with Danny Leigh, *The Guardian*, April 9, 2015.

I went through puberty in a theme park. Backstage at Disney World, there are stories. Mickey Mouse with his head off, drinking coffee on break. Pirates on the phone. Ghosts in line for food. It just made me see things.

Ryan, on spending his teenage years at Disney World, Florida, while (not) filming *The All-New Mickey Mouse Club*, interview with Tom Chiarella, *Esquire*, August 9, 2011.

66

My friends call me mouse boy.

99

Ryan, aged 12, "Canada's first ever Mouseketeer", discussing how he won his role on *The All-New Mickey Mouse Club*, interview with CTV Canada AM, 1992.

According to singer/dancer AJ McLean, Ryan was offered a spot in the now-iconic vocal group the Backstreet Boys just as they were starting out in 1993, the same time Ryan was on *The Mickey Mouse Club.*

"Long story short, we used to live in the same apartment complex when Ryan was doing *The Mickey Mouse Club.* Ryan, Justin Timberlake, Christina Aguilera and Britney Spears. We were playing basketball almost every other day. I kept telling him how big the Backstreet Boys was gonna be. He didn't think it was gonna go anywhere, and then it did. And he kinda missed the boat," McLean told Jimmy Fallon on *The Tonight Show*, February 11, 2020.

We were 12. We had natural curiosities, so we talked. I don't remember specifically what we talked about. We just talked about things the way 12-year-olds talk. We didn't know anything about sex then. I'm still not sure I know anything about it.

Ryan, on talking to Christina Aguilera, Britney Spears and other Mousketeers about sex, interview with Michael Martin, *VMAN*, September 2005.

Teaching Britney Spears about sex: Now there's an achievement! I feel somewhat responsible for how sexual she is now. When I see her with a snake around her neck, I think: Did I do that?

Ryan, on being a bad influence on Britney Spears when he was a Mouseketeer on *The All-New Mickey Mouse Club* alongside Britney Spears, Christina Aguilera and Justin Timberlake, interview with Gaby Wood, *The Guardian*, February 18, 2007.

"

You leave *The Mickey Mouse Club*, and you have this work ethic you can apply to anything. So, I moved out to Los Angeles. It's the classic story of not eating for a year and a half and waiting for the right thing.

"

Ryan, on leaving Disney and moving to L.A., interview with Anderson Jones, E! Online, October 22, 2013.

> **"**
>
> Working at the paper mill in Cornwall – that's what was on the cards for me. So I was really just trying to keep acting somehow, to see if there was something else I could do instead.
>
> **"**

Ryan, on his desire to not work at his hometown's local paper mill, the main employer for most of his family, interview with Alex Nino Gheciu, *Sharp* magazine, April 27, 2016.

"

Canada was frozen solid.
So I thought: This isn't right.
I'm moving to California
as soon as I can drive.
And that's what I did.

"

Ryan, on moving from Canada to California on his
own at the age of 16 after he left *The All-New Mickey
Mouse Club,* interview with Steve Carrell, *Interview,*
October 7, 2010.

I did the TV show *Breaker High* in Canada, which was over 200 episodes of television, so I got really great training. When I finished that, I was 16 and I moved to L.A. I was an extra in *Remember the Titans*, had two lines but was in every scene, and got to watch Denzel Washington work.

Ryan, on how he went from the *Mickey Mouse Club* to his first film roles, interview with Michael Martin, *VMAN*, September 2005.

"

I lay in bed, I stared at the phone, and I remember thinking, 'If that phone rings, my whole life will change. And if it doesn't, I'm going home.' So I was staring at it, it rang, and they said, 'You got the part!'

"

Ryan, on being totally broke and living alone in L.A. when he got the lead role in *Young Hercules* (1998–1999), interview with Ramin Setoodeh, *Variety*, February 7, 2024.

CHAPTER
TWO

Mr Nice Guy

As the light of a new millennium illuminated a new dawn, Ryan too was riding high on his second big break.

He had cleared the jump from "mouse boy" on the small screen and hit the ground running in Hollywood, landing increasingly larger roles in independent and smaller-budget movies.

He had bided his time, but was this bright star ready to shine?

When I was a kid, I had a single mom and she was very beautiful. And to me, as a young man, all men felt like wolves and there was a very threatening, predatory tone to the world in general, not just to specific people. It felt like life could become a nightmare at any second.

Ryan, on his mom, Donna, and men, interview with Alice Wasley, *Daily Telegraph Australia*, June 7, 2015.

My mom gave me the power to control my own destiny. She really encouraged me to change things I didn't like. On *The Mickey Mouse Club*, whatever problems the kids were having, most parents were so terrified that their kid would lose his position on the show that they just bowed down to Disney. But not my mother; she got right in their face about it. She taught me not to submit to any kind of arbitrary authority and gave me permission to question my teachers and the school system. It taught me that I could do that in life.

Ryan, on his mom, Donna, and her influence, interview with *SBS Australia*, May 14, 2009.

At 16 I don't think you have any sense of your own mortality, you're just operating on instinct. I came out to L.A., I don't know why. I just did. And when I was younger I had worked with a woman who was one of my first agents. I called her up, and we started talking and she started sending me out on auditions.

Ryan, on moving to Los Angeles on his own when he was just 16, interview with Luaine Lee, *Deseret News*, June 27, 2004.

66

It's very hard coming from kids' television to break the stigma. All you have is a VHS tape of you humping stuff on *The Mickey Mouse Club* and wearing fake tanner and fighting imaginary sphinxes.

99

Ryan, on his lack of dramatic experience on his Hollywood resumé after leaving *The Mickey Mouse Club* and *Young Hercules*, interview with Dennis Lim, *New York Times*, September 14, 2011.

There's something wrong when you have a grown man calling a kid 'Sir'. That fucks with your head.

Ryan, on the perils of being a successful child actor, interview with Gaby Wood, *The Guardian*, February 18, 2007.

I've always been a little more confident than my talent warranted. I've got a 'fake it 'til you make it' philosophy.

Ryan, on his unearned confidence, interview with Alice Wasley, *Daily Telegraph Australia*, June 7, 2015.

I just wanted to have more control over my life. And I thought the entertainment business, being an actor, seemed like the answer. It seemed like you make lots of money and nobody tells you what to do. I didn't realize that, with the kind of movies I was going to make, I wasn't going to make a lot of money and everyone was going to tell me what to do.

Ryan, on the movie industry when you're an up-and-coming actor, interview with Alex Pappademas, *GQ*, October 9, 2007.

You try to get people to forget that you were on *The Mickey Mouse Club* and *Young Hercules* and you want to do movies now. It takes a lot of auditioning to get people to forget.

Ryan, on auditioning a lot as a teenager in the hope of escaping his Disney child-star past, interview with Luaine Lee, *Deseret News*, June 27, 2004.

A friend was auditioning for *The Believer*… Henry Bean, the director, is crazy and likes to piss people off, so he hired the guy who was the worst choice – me. I was 19, from Canada, not Jewish, and had never done a film of that nature. I think Henry just liked that I was the dark horse.

Ryan, on being a former Disney star selected to play a Jewish Nazi in *The Believer*, interview with Michael Martin, *VMAN*, September 2005.

I was gift-wrapped my career by director Henry Bean, who gave me this opportunity to do this movie, *The Believer*… It was something that gave me the opportunity to break out [of that] in a way that I don't think I could have done without that opportunity. It was sort of as if I couldn't get an audition for *The Believer* or a movie like that, because of my Disney past.

Ryan, on his big break in dramatic roles with *The Believer* in 2001, interview with Matthew Schuchman, Den of Geek, March 30, 2013.

I had no idea then what it was exactly that I was going to do with my career. And the script for *The Believer* came along, and for some reason, in a way that I could not articulate, I knew this film was something I had to do. And I didn't know why, but I knew I wouldn't understand until I did it.

Ryan, on deciding to portray a Jewish Nazi in the movie *The Believer*, his first dramatic role after *Breaker High* and *Young Hercules*, interview with Rebecca Carroll, *The Independent*, September 1, 2005.

You know, sometimes you just want to go to the Caribbean and make a movie about pirates. And the people who make those movies have the greatest time ever, and the stories they tell are fantastic. But for me, making something like *The Believer* is more fun, because when I leave it, it gives me a bit more perspective on myself, and that settles me.

Ryan, on *The Believer* and wanting to make films that help him evolve personally and professionally, interview with Rebecca Carroll, *The Independent*, September 1, 2005.

I did a movie called *The Believer* and I suddenly found myself at Sundance, where people were asking me about my craft. So I had to pretend I had one.

Ryan, on the hype surrounding Ryan's performance in his breakout dramatic role, *The Believer*, interview with Steve Carrell, *Interview*, October 7, 2010.

Sometimes I think that the one thing I love most about being an adult is the right to buy candy whenever and wherever I want.

Ryan, on candy,* interview with Tom Chiarella, *Esquire*, August 9, 2011.

* His favourite is Twizzlers, FYI, according to Emma Stone.

It's good being an actor because if anything goes wrong you can blame it on everyone else.

Ryan, on the benefits to being an actor, interview with Michael Martin, *VMAN*, September 2005.

I really liked making *The Notebook*. Nick [Cassavetes, the director] and I felt that we really wanted to make a movie about a guy who loves his girl, that showed that men can be romantic. We need romance, too. That made Nick and me feel good because we're kind of saps. We like that mushy stuff. We don't like to admit it, but we do.

Ryan, on finding love at the movies, interview with Michael Martin, *VMAN*, September 2005.

The director Nick Cassavetes told me there was this romantic lead in *The Notebook*, but the character's fucking crazy. He writes a girl a letter every day for 365 days and builds a house that they went to once. And Nick said, 'You're crazy, you can do this.' And I was like, erm, 'Thanks?'

Ryan, on being offered to play the lead role as Noah Calhoun in *The Notebook*, interview with Jonathan Dean, *The Sunday Times*, April 28, 2024.

The *Notebook* director Nick Cassavetes straight up told me: 'The fact that you have no natural leading-man qualities is why I want you to be my leading man.'

Ryan Gosling, on becoming a leading man for the first time in *The Notebook* (2004), interview with Zach Baron, *GQ*, May 31, 2023.

I don't know if everlasting love is something you can believe in or not. I think it does exist for some people, and for others it doesn't. It's not something you're entitled to and not something that's going to happen to everybody. There are those who have it happen to them, so in that case, I guess it exists.

Ryan, on love (like you see it in the movies), interview with Luaine Lee, *Deseret News*, June 27, 2004.

God bless *The Notebook.* It introduced me to one of the great loves of my life. But people do Rachel and me a disservice by assuming we were anything like the people in that movie. Rachel's and my love story is a hell of a lot more romantic than that… the only thing I remember is we both went down swingin' and we called it a draw.

Ryan Gosling, on his real-life love with co-star Rachel McAdams after *The Notebook* had completed filming, interview with Zach Baron, *GQ*, May 31, 2023.

We inspired the worst in each other. It was a strange experience, making a love story and not getting along with your co-star in any way.

Ryan, on the infamously fiery relationship he shared with co-star Rachel McAdams* during the filming of *The Notebook*, interview with Alice Fisher, *Observer*, January 9, 2011.

* "We weren't throwing Ming vases at each other, so it wasn't loathing, but our relationship was not what you saw on the screen," McAdams said of their turbulent time making the movie, *The Times*, 2013.

We started a band, because at the time me and my friend [Zach Shields] were dating sisters [Rachel and Kayleen McAdams]. So we were the boyfriends and we spent all this time together and we were like, 'Why are we wasting our lives hanging out? Let's be productive and start a band.' We called ourselves Dead Man's Bones. We have a MySpace page.

Ryan, on his band, Dead Man's Bones, movies.ie, March 2007. The group released their first and only album in October 2009.

After seeing *The Notebook*,
they all want me to build
them a house. Which
is fine, but I can't build
that many houses.

Ryan, when asked "Is there any downside to being
famous when it comes to getting women?", interview
with Michael Martin, *VMAN*, September 2005.

Women are mad at me. A girl came up to me on the street and she almost smacked me. Like, 'How could you let a girl like that go!'

Ryan, on his and Rachel McAdam's decision to end their relationship, interview with Alex Pappademas, *GQ*, October 9, 2007.

I don't become characters.
They're all me.

Ryan, on being himself when in character, even the
oddball screw-ups, interview with Rebecca Winters
Keegan, *Time*, October 4, 2007.

Gosling.

While the word Gosling is known commonly as the term for a young goose, the name Gosling likely comes from the Old Germanic word *Gozzelin* that means "Little God".

Perfect for Ryan.

It's not like people looked at me and thought: Here's a movie star. Most of my life I've tried to prove people wrong about me, and now I kind of have to prove some people right.

Ryan Gosling, on *Half Nelson*. His performance earned him much rave praise by his peers, interview with Gaby Wood, *The Guardian*, February 18, 2007.

I really like making little movies, but the downside is that when you're making them, you're pretty sure no one's going to see them. So the Oscar nomination in some way affirms those choices by making it possible for people to hear about a film and maybe see a movie they wouldn't have otherwise seen.

Ryan, on his first Academy Award nomination for *Half Nelson* (2006), interview with Steve Carrell, *Interview*, October 7, 2010.

In 2006, Ryan became the
seventh-youngest actor
ever to be nominated
for the Academy Award
for Best Actor for his
outstanding performance
as a crack-addicted teacher
in *Half Nelson*.

He was just 25 when he
made the film.

"

Everyone's like 'Wow, you really slummed it on *Half Nelson*.' For two months of work I made way more than my dad would make in a year working at a paper mill. You get all this credit for slumming it in the indie world. It's bullshit. Actors make good money.

"

Ryan, on earning money for acting, interview with Rebecca Winters Keegan, *Time*, October 4, 2007.

It's not like I set out to be 'the indie guy'. I really believe my films are going to be successful, that I'm making the next *The Blair Witch Project* – something that will transcend expectations and resonate with people. When my films don't do well, I'm hurt and surprised. It's discouraging.

Ryan, on his films underperforming with his fans and the box office, interview with Alice Fisher, *Observer*, January 9, 2011.

You know how sometimes department stores have these things where, if you win, you get 10 minutes and go in and take anything you want from the store? That's basically what I'm doing. I'm running in and just trying to grab as many characters as possible before they pull the plug on me.

Ryan, on living his 15 minutes of fame to the fullest, interview with Neil Norman, *The Independent*, April 22, 2007.

Lars and the Real Girl is about a man who falls in love with a sex doll. It's a really beautiful love story about their relationship, and in a way it's probably closer to *The Notebook* than anything I've done.

Ryan, on the similarities between his characters in *Lars and the Real Girl* and *The Notebook*, interview with Steven Weintraub, *Collider*, April 3, 2007.

My poor mother, she doesn't ask questions anymore. She just says, 'Oh yeah, sex-doll movie. That's great!' She's a really supportive mom.

Ryan Gosling, on his mother, and his indie/offbeat film choices, interview with Matt Mueller, *The Guardian*, March 14, 2008.

I cried at the end, when I read it.
I just thought it was so romantic
– the idea that you don't need
to be loved in return in order
to love something or someone.
Love can come from you. It
doesn't have to be reciprocal.
People love their cars. People
love all kinds of things, and they
really love them…

And we don't really value that kind of love because it's not a real, reciprocal kind of love, but it's real love to them.

99

Ryan, on love and Lars's love for Bianca in *Lars and the Real Girl*, interview with Alex Pappademas, *GQ*, October 9, 2007.

66

You can't make a movie for everybody. You can't go into it trying to alienate people, but you have to assume that you're going to.

99

Ryan Gosling, on the cult success of *Lars and the Real Girl*, interview with Jack Foley, Indie London, August 26, 2011.

"

Doesn't everybody feel like an outsider? I mean, we all do. We all have trouble connecting and communicating who you think you are and relating that to who you are and people's perceptions of who you are. It's difficult to be a person.

"

Ryan Gosling, on the similarities between him and his character Lars from *Lars and the Real Girl* and his own social anxieties, interview with Matt Mueller, *The Guardian*, March 14, 2008.

I've always been surprised at how many opportunities I've gotten out of the things I really believed in, versus the things I thought I should be doing.

Ryan, on his earliest film choices borne out of a desire to make quality movies and not money, interview with Alex Pappademas, *GQ*, October 9, 2007.

Ryan's Highest Rated Films*

1. *Drive* – 93%

2. *La La Land* – 91%

3. *The Nice Guys* – 91%

4. *Half Nelson* – 91%

5. *The Big Short* – 89%

6. *Barbie* – 88%

7. *Blade Runner 2049* – 88%

8. *First Man* – 87%

9. *Blue Valentine* – 87%

10. *The Ides of March* – 83%

* According to rottentomatoes.com, May 2024.

Somebody once gave me the advice, 'Your job is just to feel it. It doesn't matter if anyone else does.' But I think having done a lot of that, I realise my job is for other people to feel it. And it's cool if I do, but that's really not the point. The point is that other people do.

Ryan, on changing his approach to acting, and no longer inhabiting characters as deeply as he once did, interview with Zach Baron, *GQ*, May 31, 2023.

66

The internet is just an abstract place. Sure, I've become part of that in some way, but it's hard for me to wrap my head around a lot of it. I prefer just to kind of stay out of it.

99

Ryan, on the internet and the millions of viral memes involving Ryan that cause a stir on social media, interview with Chris Heath, *GQ*, December 12, 2016.

CHAPTER
THREE

La La Man

Throughout the 2010s, Ryan cemented his feet in Hollywood's walk of fame as one of the most outstanding character actors of his generation, lending his name to a pedigree of movies that not only kickstarted a buzz but also a cultural conversation.

In a few short years Ryan went from driver to gangster to bank robber to jazz pianist to private detective to replicant to first man on the moon without breaking a sweat. His status as *La La Land*'s leading man was assured.

The only question that remained was, who would he become next?

I don't think it's really about me. I think it really is sort of like, I'm a pigeon and the internet is Fabio* and it just happened.

Ryan, on the "Hey Girl" viral social media memes, interview with Alex Nino Gheciu, *Sharp Magazine*, April 27, 2016.

* On March 13, 1999, male supermodel Fabio was riding a rollercoaster when, now rather infamously, a goose flew fatally into his face, severely bloodying Fabio. It's on YouTube.

In 2013, a series of short videos called "Ryan Gosling Won't Eat His Cereal" went viral on Vine and other social media platforms for many years.

The memes featured various clips from Ryan's films with a spoonful of cereal superimposed over the footage, and Ryan turning away from it, disinterested.

When the creator of the memes, Ryan McHenry, passed away in May 2015 from cancer, Ryan paid tribute to him by filming himself pour a bowl of cereal and, finally, eating it. It went viral, naturally.

> **"**
>
> I don't know enough about manliness to define it. I'm not an authority on it.
>
> **"**

Ryan, when asked to define masculinity, interview with Jessica Grose, *Slate Magazine*, July 25, 2011.

I think like a girl. I was raised by my mother and my sister. And I just feel like I wouldn't know how to think any other way. My sister was my best friend and my hero growing up. Because I was home-schooled I didn't have a lot of friends and I did ballet, which was always just girls. All of that had an effect on my brain.

Ryan, on his childhood and being raised by women, interview with Lesley O'Toole, *The Independent*, October 25, 2011.

I'd say 49 per cent, sometimes 47 per cent, it depends on what day you catch me.

Ryan, when asked what percentage woman he thought he was, interview with Stefanie Rafanelli, *The Standard*, June 3, 2016.

I had to go get a physical after I did *Blue Valentine*. For no particular reason, just that I needed a check-up. My doctor wrote me a prescription, and on it, it said, 'Do a comedy.' So I took his advice and I feel better.

Ryan, on his breakout comedy role as Jacob Palmer in *Crazy, Stupid, Love* (2011), interview with Jessica Grose, *Slate Magazine*, July 25, 2011.

I can't tell you how many times people go, 'Are you Ryan?' And I go, 'Yeah.' And they say, 'Can I get a picture?' Then they take the picture and realize, in that moment, that I'm not Ryan Reynolds. I can see the disappointment in their faces.

Ryan, on being constantly mistaken for fellow Canadian actor Ryan Reynolds, interview with Steve Carrell, *Interview*, October 7, 2010.

"

Taking some time out meant I had some experience of normal life that you can then reflect in a movie. It's not good just to have life experience of film-making and that's all. It's hard to play a real person when you've been in jets and town cars for three years.

"

Ryan, on his "fat and unemployed" break from acting after being replaced in Peter Jackson's *The Lovely Bones* in 2009 due to his being too young to play a grieving father and 60lbs overweight, interview with Emma Jones, *The Independent*, January 11, 2013.

66

We had this awful first date where we had nothing to say, and we didn't really look at one another. I got the check early and was stuck giving him a ride home to Santa Monica. So I drove him out there and he didn't talk, so I turned on the radio, and REO Speedwagon's 'I Can't Fight This Feeling Anymore' came on, and he started crying and singing this song at the top of his lungs…

And he said, 'This is the movie. It's about a guy who drives around listening to pop music.' And that's secretly what I had been feeling, so he voiced it and knew that it was right. But I never would have made *Drive* if REO Speedwagon hadn't come on the radio.

Ryan, on how he got the role of the Driver in Nicolas Winding Refn's *Drive*, interview with Jessica Grose, *Slate Magazine*, July 25, 2011.

I'm Canadian. I don't really have that much angst to get rid of.

Ryan, on becoming the Driver for Nicolas Winding Refn's *Drive*, interview with Emma Jones, *The Independent*, January 11, 2013.

I don't know how much preparation actually makes its way in obvious ways into a film. Someone else could have built a '73 Chevy Malibu and you'd never know the difference. My character [the Driver] never has to talk about cars or do anything underneath a car, so it doesn't really matter. But it felt important to me. And with every character you play, you have to find a way in.

Ryan, on building from scratch a '73 Chevy Malibu in preparation for his role of the Driver in *Drive* (2011), interview with Damon Wise, *Empire*, September 2011.

I'm just so sick of myself.
I can't imagine how everyone
else feels. And there's just
nowhere to go but down
really from here. So, hey, it's
been nice. It's been real.

Ryan, on appearing in six films in two years at the height
of his breaking into Hollywood, interview with Lesley
O'Toole, *The Independent*, October 25, 2011.

I'm in a committed relationship with film. I'm giving as much to it as a marriage. I had two of the greatest girlfriends of all time [Sandra Bullock and Rachel McAdams]. I haven't met anyone who could top them.

Ryan, on his famous ex-girlfriends and his dedication to cinema when asked "Do you mind being an object of desire?", interview with *The Times*, September 16, 2011.

I loved making this movie. Initially, I just thought I got to rob banks on a bike, but actually it goes much, much deeper than that.

Ryan, on making 2012's *The Place Beyond the Pines*, interview with Will Lawrence, *The Telegraph*, April 4, 2013.

I'm just compelled to make very violent films right now. I don't really know why.

Ryan, on his run of violent movies, including *The Place Beyond the Pines*, *Drive*, *Gangster Squad* and *Only God Forgives*, interview with Dennis Lim, *New York Times*, September 14, 2011.

I'd like to do something a little lighter. I've been in a dark place for the past couple of years. So, maybe a comedy about puppies. Flowers and puppies.

Ryan, on his darker role selection during the first half of his Hollywood career, interview with Kevin Spacey, *Interview*, January 9, 2013.

I think anybody can act. Lots of people act in their lives. There are great performances by people who've never acted before – movies are full of them. Often I think the better-known you become, the worse an actor you become at the same time. You get good at manipulating, and that's not as interesting.

Ryan, on acting and working hard to not manipulate his audience, interview with Luaine Lee, *Deseret News*, June 27, 2004.

If a movie I make makes some money, it'll just be icing on the cake. I've become comfortable with the term box-office poison. I'm cool with it. Some people make money on their movies, and some people don't. Josh Hartnett can be in anything, and it'll make $40 million. I make something, and if it makes $10, we're lucky. That's just how it goes.

Ryan, on his earliest independent films being considered unprofitable, interview with Anderson Jones, E! Online, October 22, 2013.

I spent lots of time working out the physical comedy. It's not something I've done a lot of, but it's something I've always wanted to do. I didn't shadow a private eye or anything… but maybe I'll just say that I did.

Ryan, on shifting from dramatic to comedic roles with *The Nice Guys*, and the preparations he made (or not) for the role, interview with Alex Nino Gheciu, *Sharp Magazine*, April 27, 2016.

I thought that the old Hollywood musical was a thing of the past… Although I grew up watching them, I didn't think it was something I would necessarily have an opportunity to make. *La La Land* felt special to us while we were making it…

We understood what a unique opportunity it was. It's been a real surprise to see the response to the film and how much it's resonating with the audience. I never could have expected that.

Ryan, on *La La Land* and its impact on fans and culture, interview with *Holmes Place Wellness* magazine, 2016.

I've loved and been proud of films before that, for whatever reason, weren't met with a mutual reception… It was a win to be able to make *La La Land* and to make it the way we wanted. That was enough. The fact that audiences have received it the way they have was more than enough

Ryan, on *La La Land's* critical and commercial praise and enduring legacy, interview with Pamela McClintock, *Hollywood Reporter*, February 10, 2017.

66

I think it's a cynical time and this movie has nothing to do with that.

99

Ryan, on the unbridled positivity and joy of *La La Land*, interview with Chris Heath, *GQ*, December 12, 2016.

The hardest scene to shoot in *La La Land* was the very first scene I shot. I play a complicated piano piece in one take. I had only been playing the piano for three months. Damien brought in a hand double, but I knew his dream was to shoot it without one....

I was able to do it, but it was really sort of trial by fire. There were many challenges still ahead, but it was nice to have one of them under our belt on day one.

"

Ryan, on filming the first of many of *La La Land's* musical sequences involving both advanced dancing techniques and jazz piano playing, interview with Pamela McClintock, *Hollywood Reporter*, February 10, 2017.

My favourite scene to shoot in *La La Land* is the opening number. All those dancers were dancing on the freeway, and all I had to do was sit in my car and watch. I had a front-row seat, and there was no danger of me souring the deal.

Ryan, on the awesome "Another Day of Sun" opening song, interview with Pamela McClintock, *Hollywood Reporter*, February 10, 2017.

66

In what other job is it a part of your job to just sit behind a piano for three months and play?

99

Ryan, on the perks of being a professional thespian, and *La La Land*, interview with *Ocean Blue World*, September 1, 2017.

Most of the time I'm playing brooding or very troubled, quiet kinds of guys. I often take my work and myself too seriously, so getting to do *La La Land* was a great way for me to be able to get to talk a lot, open up more, and make people laugh and enjoy themselves.

Ryan, on *La La Land*, and transforming his craft once again in a new film genre, interview with Will Stroude, *Attitude*, January 13, 2017.

I know a lot of actors talk about being in character and taking it home, but that doesn't feel right for me. I think you are all of your characters in some way and you just turn up the parts of you that are them and you turn down the parts of you who aren't.

Ryan, on method acting, and his own "fine-tuning process" of inhabiting a character, interview with Steven Weintraub, *Collider*, April 3, 2007.

Bring your mom.

Ryan, when asked "Any advice for a first-time Oscar nominee?", interview with Pamela McClintock, *Hollywood Reporter*, February 10, 2017.

In 2017, Ryan went viral (again) with the now-classic "Papyrus" sketch from one of his legendary turns on *Saturday Night Live*. In the skit, Ryan obsesses – literally goes insane – over the fact that *Avatar*, "the giant international blockbuster", used the common Papyrus font as its logo. It's Ryan in a nutshell, and so funny.

The sketch has now been seen more than 22 million times, and was revisited in a second sketch in May 2024. A must-see.

> 66
>
> I know people are
> surprised I've made it.
> But it's the movie
> I wanted to make.
>
>

Ryan, on his directorial debut, *Lost River* (2015), interview with Danny Leigh, *The Guardian*, April 9, 2015. It was not well received.

"

We were just doing a fight scene
and it just happened. But what was
funny was, when it was over, they
brought ice for my face, and Harrison
pushed me out of the way and stuck
his fist in the ice. As soon as it
happened, the director came up to
me and said, 'Look at it this way –
you just got hit by Indiana Jones.'

"

Ryan, on accidently being punched in the face by co-star
Harrison Ford during the filming of *Blade Runner 2049*
(2017), interview with Chris Heath, *GQ*, December 12,
2016.

$2 billion

The number of U.S. dollars
Ryan's films have made since
he began his tenure as a
leading man in *The Notebook*
(2004) – 20 years ago!

"

I did start acting very young but I'm glad I did, because I didn't have the fear of failure. If I'd waited until I was a little older, I might've been a lot more self-conscious, or afraid of failing.

"

Ryan, on starting acting at an early age, interview with *Glasgow Times*, April 16, 2015.

I really admire people who are doing things and saying things that I'm not – I want to be around that and learn where that comes from. So I meet these people who are real individuals, who are great at what they do and I want to figure out how to be that.

Ryan, on his love of making interesting and complex movies, and the people who make them, interview with Rebecca Carroll, *The Independent*, September 1, 2005.

"

Don't go on the cover of *GQ* and ask everyone to leave you alone. As soon as you do you're provoking it. It's my own damn fault.

"

Ryan, on media intrusion and the invasion of fame, interview with Alex Pappademas, *GQ*, October 9, 2007.

I crave connection and common ground, and movies can do that. You know, we may disagree on a lot, but we all like *Jaws*. And, predominantly, I want something to be entertaining. You can sneak in a message, but people have really important things happening in their lives, so it is important that they have fun first.

Ryan, on wanting to entertain an audience, interview with Jonathan Dean, *The Sunday Times*, April 28, 2024.

I'm making a movie with Damien about astronaut Neil Armstrong. It's one of the reasons why I met up with him initially. Then we ended up talking about musicals all night. I was deep into the genre. I had been developing a movie about Busby Berkeley for a long time and was curious about how he was going to go about making *La La Land*. It wasn't until six months later that I got an email from him asking if I still knew how to dance.

Ryan, on how he landed the lead role of Sebastian Wilder in *La La Land*, interview with Pamela McClintock, *Hollywood Reporter*, February 10, 2017.

CHAPTER
FOUR

The Kenadian

As you already know, 2023 belonged to Ryan Gosling.

Not only did he manage to beach off the whole world with his acclaimed performance as Ken, Barbie's (wannabe) boyfriend in the billion-dollar blockbuster *Barbie*, he also proved that as an actor he can do it all – comedy, violence, romance, action, drama, sci-fi, thriller – all while being a doting father and husband.

No one else is more Ken than Ryan. And, yet, he's also so much more than just Ken…

I feel very lucky to have been able to make the movies that I've made but it was all the bigger films, the action films and comedies – that made me fall in love with movies. It's those films that made me want to do this. And now it's cool to be in a phase of my life where I'm getting to make the kinds of things that inspired me to make film in general.

Ryan, on finally making the movies that inspired him to be an actor as a teenager, interview with Zach Baron, *GQ*, May 31, 2023.

The Gray Man is like the films I grew up loving. It's an escapist movie. And I really liked the character. It was like a spy who doesn't want to be a spy, who'd rather be at home watching Netflix like the rest of us.

Ryan, on *The Gray Man* (2022) and playing the character of Court Gentry, interview with Zach Seemayer, ET Online, July 12, 2022.

I think it's watching a character not give up and face incredible odds. And go through something that seems impossible and somehow make it out the other side. That's inspiring on some level. If they can do that, then I can deal with whatever my everyday life problem is.

Ryan, on the power of the action hero movie, interview with Johnny Davis, *The Times*, June 17, 2023.

Ryan is so much more than just Ken.

So, can you guess the name of the movie by any of his other characters' names?

1. Willy Beachum

2. Henry Letham

3. Sean Hanlon

4. Dean Pereira

5. Sebastian Wilder

6. Stephen Meyers

7. Dan Dunne

8. Danny Balint

9. Jared Vennett

10. Courtland Gentry

1. Fracture 2. Stay 3. Breaker High 4. Blue Valentine 5. La La Land 6. The Ides of March 7. Half Nelson 8. The Believer 9. The Big Short 10. The Gray Man

Barbie [the doll] landed in my house at the same time as the script. What was interesting to me is that my kids don't just brush their hair and dress them up. They all have complicated back stories, lives, relationships, hopes, dreams. It's incredible how intricate the world is that they've created…

They don't even call him Ken. One of them is named Darrell. And Darrell works at a grocery store. Ken is such a non-presence in their world. They were like 'What is there to play? Is there meat on that bone?'

Ryan, on his two daughters playing with Barbie and Ken dolls at home, interview with Ariana Brockington, *Today*, July 16, 2023.

There were actual reasons why I couldn't do the film. Schedule things. Life things. And I would call months later to my agent and say, 'Hey, who did they get to play Ken?' And they would say, 'Greta says it's you.'

Ryan, on originally turning down the role of Ken, only to be told by director Greta Gerwig that he couldn't refuse,* interview with Ramin Setoodeh, *Variety*, February 7, 2024.

* When Greta Gerwig wrote the *Barbie* script during lockdown, she wrote it for Gosling. His name was in the script as "Ken Ryan Gosling", even though they had never met.

The script is one of the best I've ever read. Margot and Greta are capable of anything. I felt very lucky to be part of it. It's made by a brilliant film-maker and there's a performance by Margot that's so human, for a doll, you can't imagine.

Ryan, on the brilliance of the *Barbie* movie (2023), interview with Johnny Davis, *The Times*, June 17, 2023.

My first impression was the title page of the script, which said 'Barbie and Ken' but 'and Ken' was scratched out. And my next impression was, this is the hardest part I'll ever play. How do you approach playing a 70-year-old crotchless doll?

There's no research you can do for that. There's no one you can shadow, no documentaries you can watch, no books written about Ken. You're on your own.

Ryan, when asked "What was your first impression of the part of Ken?", interview with Lynn Hirschberg, *W Magazine*, January 3, 2024.

My children's interest in Barbie and their disinterest in Ken was an inspiration. They were already making little movies about their Barbies on the iPad when I got the role, so the fact that I was going off to work to make one too, we just felt like we were aligned.

Ryan, on his children as inspiration to finally agree to portray Ken in *Barbie*, interview with Ellen Gamerman, *Wall Street Journal*, May 2, 2024.

> **"**
> I did see him face down
> in the mud outside one
> day, next to a squished
> lemon, and it was like…
> this guy's story does need
> to be told, you know?
> **"**

Ryan Gosling, on his decision to portray Ken in *Barbie* after watching his daughters abandon the Ken doll at home, interview with Zach Baron, *GQ*, May 31, 2023.

Eventually, I thought, 'Who am I to argue with Greta Gerwig and Margot?' They had a vision for it. They believed it. And they believed I should do it more than I believed I shouldn't.

Ryan, on finally accepting the role of Ken, but only because of Greta Gerwig and Margot Robbie's persistence, interview with Ramin Setoodeh, *Variety*, February 7, 2024.

66

I would say, you know, if people don't want to play with my Ken, there are many other Kens to play with.

99

Ryan, on the negative press and online hate he received for being "too old" to play Ken when the news of his casting was announced, interview with Zach Baron, *GQ*, May 31, 2023.

> **"**
>
> I did doubt my Kenergy in the beginning. I just wasn't sure I could do it but I just decided I was going to Ken as hard as I can. I Kenned in the morning; I Kenned at night. If I'm honest, I'm Kenning a little right now.
>
> **"**

Ryan Gosling, on having the "Kenergy" to properly portray Ken in Barbie, interview with Jess Cagle, *The Jess Cagle Show*, SiriusXM, June 26, 2023.

> **"**
>
> Ken – his job is beach. For 60 years, his job has been beach. What the fuck does that even mean?
>
> **"**

Ryan, on Ken and how best to portray him despite not having much to go on, interview with Zach Baron, *GQ*, May 31, 2023.

That Ken life is, that Ken life is… It's even harder than *The Gray Man* life, I think. Ken's got no money. He's got no job. He's got no car, he's got no house. He's going through some stuff.

Ryan, on the struggles of being a Ken in a Barbie world, interview with Zach Seemayer, ET Online, July 12, 2022.

It was basically nothing. It was just, like, coffee.

Ryan, on his super-restrictive diet while filming Barbie to ensure his washboard abs were very visible, interview with Ramin Setoodeh, *Variety*, February 7, 2024.

There were moments when I left *Blue Valentine* just completely emotionally spent, laying on the floor of the car on the ride home just done – empty. And it was even harder to play Ken. And I thought, 'How am I feeling that on this film?'

Ryan, on the struggle of trying to impart some realness into his portrayal of Ken when compared to the making of the movie *Blue Valentine* with Michelle Williams, interview with Ramin Setoodeh, *Variety*, February 7, 2024.

"

So many times, I would come home and say, 'What am I doing?' And I would overthink it. But Eva would always tell me to 'just make it about Barbie'. And so every take became an opportunity to get Barbie to notice me.

"

Ryan, on his struggle to find a way to portray Ken properly and getting help from his wife, interview with Ramin Setoodeh, *Variety*, February 7, 2024.

Barbie was obviously not what I expected. It's so elegantly and brilliantly designed by Greta and Margot to be like a theme park, where you don't really need a map. I went on the ride and I'm still going on it. I don't want to leave the park. They are kicking me out. 'The park is closing, sir.' But I ordered churros and they are coming, I swear.

Ryan Gosling, on not wanting to leave the *Barbie* party following its huge cultural impact, interview with Nicole Sperling, *New York Times*, July 13, 2023.

There's a Ken in all of us, I think.

Ryan, on the importance of being Ken, interview with Johnny Davis, *The Times*, June 17, 2023.

He was wearing a tuxedo, albeit a sleeveless one. And I asked my daughters, 'What happened?' And they said, 'Oh, he died of armpit arthritis. Ken's dead!' And I was like, 'Well, at least he's face up and wearing clothes.' I feel like he was a little better off than where I found him.

Ryan, on finding his daughters looked after their Ken doll more after Ryan had portrayed him in *Barbie*, interview with Ramin Setoodeh, *Variety*, February 7, 2024.

I think Greta had more affection for Ken than any other character. Even though she made a Barbie film, she was very conscious that she has two little boys and so wanted to start a conversation. I heard about a kid whose girlfriend broke up with him and he'd watch 'I'm Just Ken' to make him feel it was OK. Like, 'I just wasn't the right person for her, but that doesn't mean there is anything wrong with me.'

Ryan, on the power and his portrayal of the Ken in *Barbie*, interview with Jonathan Dean, *Sunday Times*, April 28, 2024.

I care about this dude now.
I'm like his representative.
'Ken couldn't show up to
receive this award, so I'm
here to accept it for him.'

Ryan, on caring about Ken, interview with Zach Baron,
GQ, May 31, 2023.

"

Kenergy is like Wi-Fi. It's there, but, do you know how it's really there? I don't. I mean – could you explain Wi-Fi?

"

Ryan, trying to explain Kenergy to a room fill of journalists, *Barbie* Canadian Press Day, Toronto, Ontario, June 28, 2023.

Very little is known about Kenergy. And we don't have the funding for the research. We know that it's real. In my case it came on as a rash, and then it turned into a tan. And then suddenly you're shaving your legs, and you're bleaching your hair, and you're wearing bespoke rollerblades.

Ryan, on his Kenergy, how he got it, and how he now can't get rid of it, interview with Zosha Millman, *Polygon*, December 12, 2023.

What is Kenergy, other than a word I made up on a press junket so I didn't have to answer questions that will haunt me the rest of my life? Well, it's a noun and I've come to understand it as the strength and vitality required to sustain a period of Kenning. What is Kenning, you ask? You didn't ask? Well, it's a verb. To Ken, it's to do more than is necessary, or required, to reflect so that others might shine.

Ryan, in a speech on Ken, Kenergy and Kenning, *Variety* Hitmakers Brunch, December 9, 2023.

It's an honour to have your work acknowledged, but for Ken, this is the first time he's been acknowledged, for anything, EVER!

Ryan, on helping get Ken some kind of recognition (finally!), interview with Lynn Hirschberg, *W Magazine*, January 3, 2024.

What would young Ryan say? First of all, I'd be like, 'Hey, young Ryan, calm down.' Then I'd say, 'Don't ask how. Don't ask why; I don't have time. But you're gonna be in a Barbie movie.'

Ryan, when asked "What would you tell your younger self if you were to ever meet?", interview with Zach Baron, GQ, May 31, 2023.

It can't be pared down, OK? It's anthemic. So we'll need a budget.

Ryan, on the one condition to agree to perform "I'm Just Ken" at the 2024 Academy Awards, interview with Ramin Setoodeh, *Variety*, February 7, 2024.

Ryan Gosling's live performance of his Oscar-nominated song "I'm Just Ken" at the 2024 Academy Awards is already considered one of the most iconic moments in Oscars history.

Dressed head-to-toe in sparkly neon pink, Ryan stole the show with Guns N' Roses guitarist Slash and Mark Ronson, alongside 65 other "Kens", and his *Barbie* co-stars.

More than 20 million people tuned in to watch and sales of the song jumped by 900 per cent during the performance.

There are a lot of cynical films about Hollywood. But we have one of the best jobs in the world, so we wanted to turn a lens onto all the people that really make these films, to honour them. They're the lifeblood. And it's never their fault if the film doesn't turn out well.

Ryan, on stunt performers and the joy of action movies such as *The Fall Guy*, interview with Jonathan Dean, *The Sunday Times*, April 28, 2024.

In *The Fall Guy* there are so many legendary stunt performers trying to break their own records. It was a really special experience to be around them and watch the risks they were taking. So much of the industry is to do with stunts. You think of Buster Keaton and Jackie Chan, and much of what inspired people to love film initially, as a medium, came from their work.

Ryan, on *The Fall Guy* and the importance of stunt performers, interview with Johnny Davis, *The Times*, June 17, 2023.

I had to pretend in that moment to be the coolest dude who's fine and not afraid of what he's doing, but I was very afraid. I think I put sunglasses on in the scene just to hide the fear.

Ryan, on *The Fall Guy*'s famous opening stunt where Ryan had to fall backwards nine stories, interview with Ben Court, *Men's Health*, April 22, 2024.

If I'm still acting at 46 I'll be surprised. How many characters can you play? I've been acting since I was 12. If I do this for ten more* years I'll be shocked.

Ryan, on the longevity of his acting career, interview with Tom Shone, *Daily Telegraph*, September 10, 2011.

* Ryan was born in 1980. Not long to go!

CHAPTER
FIVE

The Fall Guy

From eccentric indie anti-hero to big-budget blockbuster bad-ass, Ryan's fans – Goslettes? – all over the world have completely fallen in love with him. To them, they are his fall guy, a celebrity you can always rely on to deliver the goods.

As Ryan celebrates 20 years of being a leading man – not only at work, but also at home with his wife, Eva Mendes, and their two daughters – let's bask in the light of his wittiest words of wisdom and his inimitable guide to life.

So if you're feeling down today, just remember one thing: Be More Ryan.

I've learned it's important not to limit yourself. You can do whatever you really love to do, no matter what it is.

Ryan, on life lessons he's learned and manifesting his own destiny, interview with *Ocean Blue World*, September 1, 2017.

"

If you're going to take yourself out of your comfort zone and challenge yourself, you risk looking ridiculous for doing that. But it also felt worth it.

"

Ryan, on *La La Land* (2016) and his fear of looking ridiculous during the dance sequences, interview with Chris Heath, *GQ*, December 12, 2016.

Match Ryan's quote with the movie – if you can!

1. "Tell me the difference between stupid and illegal and I'll have my wife's brother arrested."

2. "You don't love me, you don't like me, I fuckin' get it. I'm a piece of shit, OK?"

3. "You shut your mouth. Or I'll kick your teeth down your throat and I'll shut it for you."

4. "You can lie, you can cheat, you can start a war, you can bankrupt the country, but you can't fuck the interns. They get you for that."

5. "Who are you, my fairy godmother? No offense, I thought you'd look different."

6. "You warned me he was smart. You didn't warn me you were stupid."

7. "I want all of you, for ever, you and me, every day."

8. "To be honest, when I found out the patriarchy wasn't just about horses, I lost interest."

9. "They were trying to kill me. And not in a fun way."

10. "I guess I'll see you in the movies."

1. The Big Short 2. The Place Beyond the Pines 3. Drive 4. The Ides of March 5. The Gray Man 6. Fracture 7. The Notebook 8. Barbie 9. The Fall Guy 10. La La Land

66

I was like, 'I can't mess this up. I can't be the guy that messed up the Barbie movie.' So if I'm going to do it, I have to do more than I know that I'm even capable of.

99

Ryan, on taking his portrayal of Ken seriously for *Barbie*, interview with Ramin Setoodeh, *Variety*, February 7, 2024.

It's the hardest role I've ever had to play. It was like a high-wire act – in tiny shorts and no shirt – with no net.

Ryan, on playing Ken in *Barbie*, interview with Ramin Setoodeh, *Variety*, February 7, 2024.

I was reacting to the audience…
It was like they were watching their
childhood homes catch fire!
I thought someone had had a heart
attack or was in danger. Then I found
out they had just read the wrong
name, and it was just funny.

Ryan, on his viral smirk 'n' giggle onstage at the 2017
Academy Award when the wrong film (*La La Land*)
was announced as winner of Best Picture instead of
Moonlight, *The Graham Norton Show*, September 28,
2018.

I thank God for music. It's made me a better actor. I think acting has made me a better musician.

Ryan, on his accomplished jazz guitar and piano playing skills, and his song writing, interview with *Ocean Blue World*, September 1, 2017.

For two summers, I watched four movies every day, and eventually, I watched so many movies, the guy behind the store counter said, 'If you really want to see something, you've got to see this.' And he gave me *Blue Velvet*. And the way it was presented to me, I loved it already. And I wanted to make things that were being passed under the table. I didn't want to be on the shelves.

Ryan, on his role selection process, interview with Jay Stone, *National Post*, September 2, 2011.

I think I was always bound to become two selves, if I wasn't already. Now there's this me and this public me. Even my own name sounds like just someone I know.

Ryan, on there being two versions of Ryan in the world, interview with Tom Chiarella, *Esquire*, August 9, 2011.

> **"** Don't let others influence you with negativity. Negativity is a killer and has stopped a lot of good people out there from pursuing their dreams. Believe in yourself. **"**

Ryan, on his life philosophy and staying positive, interview with Whitney Scott Bain, *Starburst Magazine*, 2011.

Usually, I drive like my mother. But when I'm alone, and I pass an empty parking lot, I'd be lying if I don't run through the possibilities of drifting a little and doing a few backwards 180s. Once you have that knowledge, it's hard to shake it.

Ryan, on the driving skills he learned in his preparations for the role of the Driver in *Drive*, interview with Ellen Gamerman, *Wall Street Journal*, May 2, 2024.

I think there's an idea out there that you become an actor because you like to be at the centre of attention, or because you're a natural performer… But I feel more often than not that what drives you to become an actor is an instinct to disappear. To become someone else. Not yourself.

Ryan, on the reasons and motivations behind why some actors choose the profession, interview with Chris Heath, *GQ*, December 12, 2016.

"

I feel very lucky. I've worked hard for it, but I also was lucky. I know so many talented people that have not had the same luck, and it's frustrating because they equally deserve it. It's just one of those things that you have to have that luck as well, so I'm grateful that I have.

"

Ryan, on his good fortune and hard graft, interview with *Holmes Place Wellness* magazine, 2016.

I was looking for her, you know?

Ryan, on his wife Eva Mendes, interview with Zach Baron, *GQ*, May 31, 2023.

"

I wasn't thinking about kids before I met her, but after I met Eva, I realised that I just didn't want to have kids without her. And there were moments on *The Place Beyond the Pines* where we were pretending to be a family, and I didn't really want it to be pretend anymore. I realized that this would be a life I would be really lucky to have.

"

Ryan, on having kids and his relationship with Eva Mendes, whom he met on 2012's *The Place Beyond the Pines*, interview with Zach Baron, *GQ*, May 31, 2023.

Children were not something I really thought about, or even thought I wanted. I didn't have a romanticized idea of it. It came about in a very surprising and kind of organic way. There was nothing kind of premeditated about it. It just suddenly was: My life had changed. And thank God it did.

Ryan, on having children with wife Eva Mendes, interview with Chris Heath, *GQ*, December 12, 2016.

"

I think women are better than men. They are stronger. More evolved. You can tell especially when you have daughters and you see their early stages, they are just leaps and bounds beyond boys immediately. My home life now is mostly women. They are better than us. They make me better.

"

Ryan, on women, interview with Stefanie Rafanelli, *The Standard*, June 3, 2016.

> **"**
> It kills me every time.
> There's just nothing
> – nothing – better
> than that. **"**

Ryan, on his two young daughters calling him "Papi"
("Daddy" in Spanish), interview with Ellen Gamerman,
Wall Street Journal, May 2, 2024.

"

I only know what it's like to have my kids. And in my situation, Eva's the dream mother, and they're dream babies, and it's like a dream that I'm having right now. I'm dreaming it all. So I feel so lucky.

"

Ryan, on his dreamy family with wife Eva Mendes, interview with Chris Heath, *GQ*, December 12, 2016.

When you meet your kids you realize that they deserve great parents. And then you have your marching orders and you have to try and become the person that they deserve.

Ryan, on being a good father for his two young daughters, interview with Chris Heath, *GQ*, December 12, 2016.

"

My priorities changed, and I wanted to be with my kids. I didn't want to miss anything. I hear the clock ticking. I don't know how much time I'm going to get, and I don't want to spend it in the wrong place. I know I'm not spending it in the wrong place if I'm with my family.

"

Ryan, on taking a four-year hiatus from acting when his daughters were born, interview with Ramin Setoodeh, *Variety*, February 7, 2024.

> **"**
>
> I treat acting more like work now, and not like it's therapy. It's a job, and I think in a way that allows me to be better at it because there's less interference.
>
> **"**

Ryan, on treating acting differently once he became a father, interview with Zach Baron, *GQ*, May 31, 2023.

Oh, I couldn't do *Drive* now, with my kids at the age they are. I just couldn't. So these current films work perfectly for where we are at as a family right now.

Ryan, on no longer accepting violent, edgy character roles for the sake of his children, interview with Jonathan Dean, *The Sunday Times*, April 28, 2024.

> **"**
>
> I don't really take roles that are going to put me in some kind of dark place. The decisions I make, I make them with Eva and we make them with our family in mind first.
>
> **"**

Ryan, on no longer accepting violent or dark roles without first consulting his family, interview with Ellen Gamerman, *Wall Street Journal*, May 2, 2024.

My eldest daughter was on set and I was doing a fight scene with Harrison [Ford] and she just yelled out in the middle of the take, 'You're winning!'

Ryan, on filming *Blade Runner 2049* with Harrison Ford, and taking his children to the set, interview with Chris Heath, *GQ*, December 12, 2016.

Run it by Eva first.

Ryan, when asked to "Describe the rest of your life in five words", interview with Stephen Colbert, *The Stephen Colbert Show*, May 10, 2024.

66

I make a hell of a raspberry pie. My mom used to bake as a side hustle, and I've been lucky enough to get the pie gene. I flute my crust too, so don't let anyone tell you that I don't!

99

Ryan, when asked "What is your secret skill?", interview with Lynn Hirschberg, *W Magazine*, January 3, 2024.

66

Being a celebrity is the best drug you'll ever do. Magical things happen. There's instant access to everything. As with all drugs there's a dark side, but when actors talk about the downside of fame I roll my eyes. You say you want something, it appears. The people in movies become the people you know.

99

Ryan, on fame and celebrity, interview with *The Times*, September 16, 2011.